TO VERNA
HOPE YOU ENJOY
RICHARD LEWIS

"Gee, dad, weren't we here last week?"

Yes, we probably were. I have always loved airplanes and airports and would take my family to any airport, anytime.

This photo of my son Rick was taken in 1965 at Greater Rockford Airport. The rest of the family were there too... my wife Diane, and other sons Tom and Dan.

Rick became the airport nut in the family. This book is dedicated to all of my family and all of the airport and history lovers out there.

I learned to fly here at RFD and have a soft spot for this particular airport as I have watched it grow over the years.

It was an Airport before it was an Airport!
The story of Greater Rockford Airport from Camp Grant to the present day.

Richard Lewis

Library of Congress cataloging in publication data

Lewis, Richard
      It was an airport before it was an Airport! The story of Greater Rockford
      Airport from Camp Grant to the present day.
      Richard Lewis
      Includes chronology and index
      ISBN 978-1-60461-389-6

      Cover aerial photo: Gary Chambers

      First Edition

      Printed in U.S.A. by Johnson Press

INTRODUCTION

Many of today's airports were built on unoccupied farm or ranchland. Greater Rockford Airport sits on a piece of land with quite a history. This book will try to give you the feel of this land as it progressed from farmland in 1917 to today's modern airport. Although I was planning on a very factual book about this time in history, I could not help interjecting my own thoughts and participation.

And yes, as the title says, it really *was* an airport before it was an airport: The 108 Aero Squadron was based at what was Camp Grant in 1927. These aircraft used a portion of the parade grounds for a runway. In 1938 there were even plans to build two 3,000 foot crushed rock runways. These plans were later dropped.

CAMP GRANT

1917-1921

The war in Europe had been raging since August of 1914, but with the sinking of the passenger liner Lusitania, the U.S. could no longer ignore its obligation and in April of 1917 declared war on Germany. At this time the US was severely lacking in military facilities. The decision was made to establish the necessary Military Cantonments throughout the country to handle the needs of this new war.

One of the largest was slated for the Midwest and it began to look as though an area south of Rockford, Illinois might be the location. The first indication was a headline in the Friday, June 1, 1917 Rockford Daily Register-Gazette stating: "ARMY MEN HERE TOMORROW." Then on Thursday June, 7th the headline confirmed it: "ROCKFORD TO GET CAMP." Its centralized location, railroads and rivers all contributed to the choice. The cantonment was slated for immediate construction.

The Pease home after being taken over by the Army for officers' quarters.

You can imagine the surprise and mixed feelings of the Lace, Pease, James, Johnson, and McLarty farm families when they received notice that the U.S. government was going to pay them $835,000 collectively for a little over 3000 acres of their land. *(In 2007 dollars that's almost $14 million…$4,600 per acre!)* This land was to become an integral part of the camp

We can also imagine the feelings of the people in the Rockford/New Milford area as they prepared for the influx of over 8,500 workers and the construction of 1,100 buildings in the span of five months. The initial cost of the camp would be over $7 million *(almost $125 million in 2007 dollars)* and would be built to house over 50,000 personnel. The boundaries were Sandy Hollow Road to the north, farmland to the east, Kishwaukee River to the south and the Rock River to the west. *(A "city," to house a population of what was the size of Rockford at that time, to be built in five months!)* Even today it is hard to believe it could be done.

The McLarty home in 1917.

One of the 180 barracks built by November 1917. The photo at the bottom of the page shows that many were under construction at the same time.

Construction began on July 1, 1917 and the planned first 1,100 buildings were completed by November. These included 180 barracks, latrines, mess halls, power plants and special buildings such as Red Cross buildings, YMCA buildings, Officers Club, Station Hospital, Post Office, and American Library Association facilities. The Liberty Theater, YMCA Auditorium and the Knights of Columbus Auditorium were entertainment venues with the Liberty Theater being the largest…seating 4,500.

The total area of the camp was 5,640 acres, within which eighteen miles of water pipe were laid. The camp water plant pumped 6,000,000 gallons of water per day. Three hundred and fifty miles of electric wire was strung. The 1,520 buildings had an aggregate floor space of 2,200 acres. Forty-eight million feet of lumber, 680 tons of nails and 21,000 barrels of cement were used in constructing the buildings and their foundations. In all, 4,500 carloads of material were hauled into camp by railroads. During construction, tracks were laid on the parade grounds and later removed when construction was finished

This photo emphasized the importance of having the railroads in the area with much of the material needed for the camp coming in by rail.

I have no idea what these three people are doing at the construction site, but it is an interesting photo.

Fifty-nine steam-heating plants furnished heat for the camp through a system of 32 miles of pipes. Each of the big power plants contained a battery of from two to ten 250-horsepower boilers. In contrast to the heating system, an ice plant turned out 20,000 tons of ice a day to supply the cold-storage house and the refrigerators of the 180 barracks. From these barracks fifteen tons of rubbish were carted away each day to the garbage incinerator to be burned. Most of the garbage from the camp was sold to near-by farmers for feeding to hogs.

Nothing changes... back in 1917 it still took five men to watch and one to do the job.

Once the truck was unloaded from the box car it was loaded and driven to the job site.

Steam was the order of the day for locomotion. Diesels were still 20 years away.

Greater Rockford Airport

CAMP GRANT
1917-1921 *an overview*

OFFICERS CLUB

YMCA BUILDING

YMCA AUDITORIUM

REMOUNT STATION

12

KISHWAUKEE ROAD

RED CROSS BUILDING

LIBERTY THEATER

C.B. & Q. RAILWAY DEPOT

YMCA HOSTESS HOUSE

BELL BOWL

NEW MILFORD

Early on, the Cantonment was renamed for General Ulysses S. Grant. This overview gives an indication of the layout of the camp and its relationship to today's airport (the area shown in blue.)

Since horses and mules were still used by the army, Camp Grant had a remount depot at the far south end of the camp, which had a capacity of 5,000 animals. At this station, animals for the army were assorted and assigned to the various army posts that were in the zone of the central department at Chicago. In connection with the remount depot was a school for blacksmiths. The remount area covered 15 acres.

Fire protection for the camp was secured through an efficient fire department, housed in three fire stations. Two hundred and sixty-two fire hydrants were provided throughout the camp and 18,000 pails and as many fire extinguishers were placed in the various buildings for emergency use.

CAMP GRANT PANORAMIC

This view looking southwest was taken on September 15, 1917. Notice the temporary rail lines running down what was to become the parade grounds.

This view was made later in 1917 by a Kansas City photographer.

CAMP GRANT—ROCKFORD, ILL.
RELEASED BY COMMAND OF MAJ. GEN. BARRY
CHARLES T. LULL, MAJ., G. S. C., ASST. CHIEF OF STAFF
WATERLOO PHOTOGRAPH CO., WATERLOO, IA.
PHOTOGRAPHS BY THE MILLION

Looking

VIEWS

The panoramic camera was a new phenomenon at the time and there are many panoramic photos of early Camp Grant.

CAMP GRANT

1917-1921... at ease

Baseball, football, boxing, music, reading, one of first U.S. Army Bands and, of course, girls were all part of life at Camp Grant.

Baseball game outside the barracks.

Maybe he was playing the song of the day; "Over There."

A time for song and dance.

It looks like they are using the "T" formation.

These fellows are in the enlisted men's recreation room at the hospital base.

One of the PX (Post Exchange stores).

Reading, writing letters and playing cards in the lower level of the barracks.

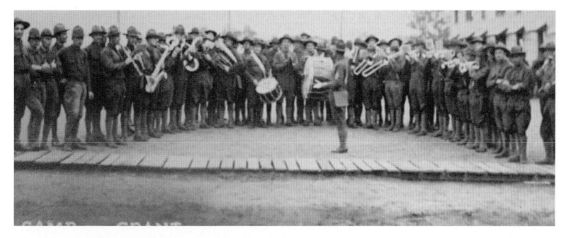

The first U.S. Army Band practicing at the Camp.

Boxing was a very popular sport at the Camp.

Studying at the Base Hospital Library.

CAMP GRANT
1917-1921... at work

From hand-to-hand combat techniques to keeping the living quarters in shape, Camp Grant offered the full range of military training.

Field mess during maneuvers.

The rifle range. The winter clad troops are shooting at targets across the frozen Kishwaukee River.

Working on the proper form to throw a hand grenade.

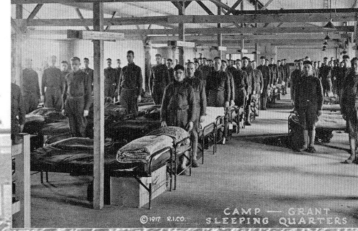

The barracks ready for inspection.

The horse artillery training in the field at Camp Grant.

Bayonet practice.

Two-man machine gun training.

Hand-to-hand combat practice.

CAMP GRANT
Hospital Unit

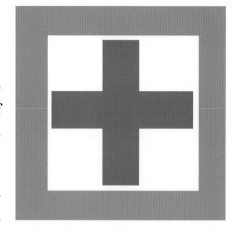

The base hospital unit, located at the far north end of the camp, contained 61 buildings, which were erected at a cost of $500,000. Thousands of dollars worth of equipment and supplies were purchased for the hospital.

The unit housed the 108th Medical Battalion. It was both a training and treatment center. The unit was severely tested with the Spanish Influenza epidemic that swept the camp in 1918. Over 1,000 men died between September 23 and October 1 of that year.

The Red Cross Building.

Most of the hospital buildings were connected with covered walkways.

The operating room.

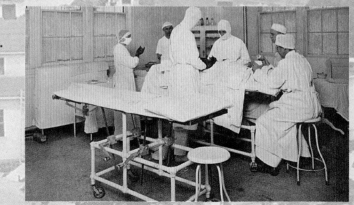

Medical Unit personnel posing by the Rock River in 1918.

Ambulances of the 108th Medical Battalion.

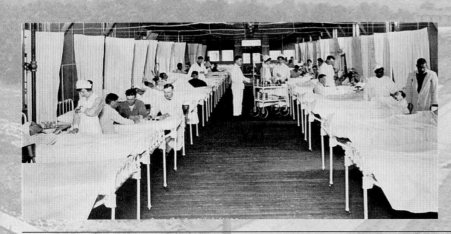

One of the sixty medical wards.

Other Camp Life

Army field communication was much more basic in 1917. The signal corps, shown practicing here, were an important part of the Army. Using flags, the arm positions would designate words or letters.

The photo just says "Army Bake Ovens." We have to gather they were wood burning and probably furnished the bread for the camp.

One of the highlights during the time of Camp Grant was a visit by former president Theodore Roosevelt on September 26, 1917. This was Roosevelt's third visit to Rockford. He had been here in 1903 as President and again in 1912 as he was running for his third term as President.

The "Colonel", as he was known, addressed 21,000 soldiers at the camp. This was part of a nationwide tour to promote the country's participation in the European Theater.

Teddy Roosevelt on tour of the camp with General Thomas Berry leading the way.

Chairs were not a luxury to be enjoyed at the new camp.

CAMP GRANT
1924-1940

With the war ending in 1918, almost all of the Camp Grant buildings were auctioned off when the base closed in 1921. In 1924 the base became the home for the Illinois National Guard. This 1939 aerial shows how empty this once bustling area had become. Distinctive features were the 1,500 concrete tent pads that were built for the National Guard and occupied the area of the 1917 barracks. A few of these pads still exist near the south end of the airport.

During the 20s and 30s, the Illinois National Guard conducted its annual training at Camp Grant. Units from all over the state would come for 15 days of training each summer. Tents were the method of housing the troops with 12'x12' concrete pads provided to avoid problems with rain or mud. This hand-colored postcard photo shows these tents and pads.

These crumbling concrete tent pads in this recent photo are some of the last remnants of Camp Grant.

CAMP GRANT
1941-1945

RECEPTION CENTER

39TH STREET

STATION HOSPITAL

BLACKHAWK ROAD

NEW MILFORD SCHOOL ROAD

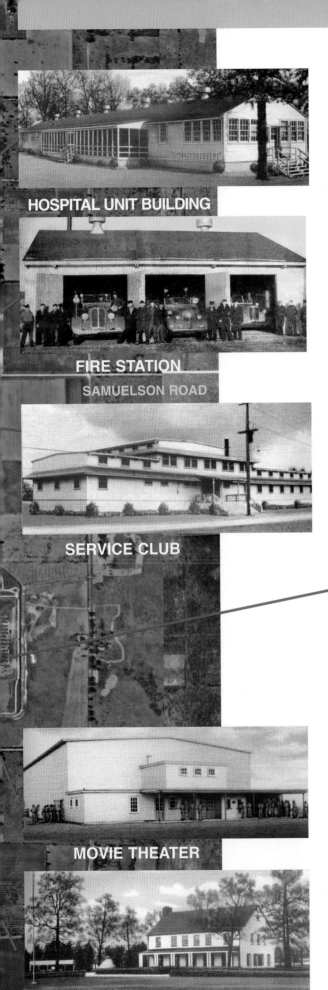

HOSPITAL UNIT BUILDING

FIRE STATION
SAMUELSON ROAD

SERVICE CLUB

MOVIE THEATER

OFFICERS CLUB

With the clouds of war again on the horizon, Camp Grant was reactivated in early 1941. Three-hundred and forty-one buildings, including 165 barracks, were built at a cost of $4,252,000. This included the Midwest Medical Replacement Training Center and a Recruit Reception Center.

The fire station shown is one of the few remaining buildings still standing today. It is now part of the Camp Grant Museum on Samuelson Road.

In 1943 a prisoner of war area was constructed. This area was intended to handle German Prisoners Of War from the Afrika Corps, Wermacht and some U-boat sailors. While they were at Camp Grant these POWs worked off site at canneries and farms for 80 cents a day. There were no escapees from 1943 until the end of the war.

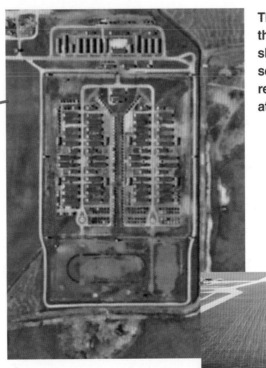

This close-up view of the POW compound shows the barracks, security fence and recreation area at the south.

This current view looking south from Kishwaukee and 39th St. (Airport Dr.) shows another remnant of the old camp; it is what is left of Kishwaukee St. as it once extended to Samuelson Road.

CAMP GRANT
1941-1945

The second Camp Grant was known as the largest gateway to the Great National Army. It was also the Midwest Medical Replacement Center.

Getting their dress uniforms.

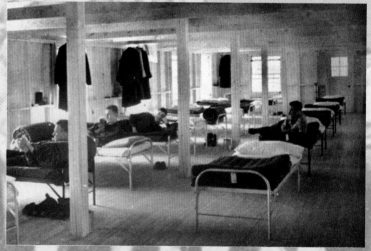

Relaxing in the barracks.

On maneuvers at the south end
of the camp.

U. S. POST OFFICE, CAMP GRANT, ILLINOIS

POST OFFICE
CAMP GRANT BRANCH
ROCKFORD P.O.

T-524

Hand-colored postcard
showing the camp post
office and barracks.

The post exchange at a busy
time.

CAMP GRANT
1941-1945

Incoming raw recruits arriving at the C.B. & Q. railway depot.

This aerial view shows that the World War II Camp Grant occupied only a small part of what was the World War I camp.

Dancing at the service club.

Ambulance crew practicing in the field.

After thirteen weeks of training the raw recruits are sent to their next destination as soldiers.

Rockford Airport... The Beginning

Although the quality is not very good, this rare aerial photo of Machesney Field shows North Second Street in the upper left and a full parking lot.

Greetings from
ROCKFORD, ILLINOIS
"Illinois' Second Industrial City"
Commemorating the first flight of
AIR MAIL SERVICE
from ROCKFORD
Send your CORRESPONDENCE *and* EXPRESS
VIA AIR MAIL
and TRAVEL VIA AIR
to ROCKFORD, ILLINOIS
Now Connecting with
All Direct U. S. AIR MAIL ROUTES

This Card is Sent by Air Mail ~ For Speed, Reply by Air Mail

A postcard promoting the Rockford Air Mail Service.

Another photo of a rare airplane shot at Machesney Field. It looks to be an Army trainer, circa 1935, but I can't definitely identify.

No history of aviation in Rockford would be complete without reference to Machesney Field. Started by barnstormer Fred Machesney in 1927, it was located northeast of Rockford. The field was known as "Rockford's Airport" and obtained airmail service in 1930. Even though privately owned, Machesney Field served as the city's airport until the construction of Greater Rockford Airport.

The Rockford Chamber of Commerce and the City Council fought against it, but the Greater Rockford Airport Committee won out, and in 1946, President Harry Truman deeded the land that was Camp Grant to the Greater Rockford Airport Authority. This fight for an airport was just the beginning of a rocky relationship over the years between the city and the Greater Rockford Airport Authority (GRAA).

The committee made this simplistic plea to the community with this poster.

Greater Rockford Airport
1951

The northern boundary of the new airport was 39th Avenue with the Rock River on the west, Kishwaukee River on the south and rail tracks to the east. There was a total of 1600 acres along with 14 buildings and 31 warehouses. Also, this year, the first meeting of the GRAA Board of Commissioners was held in the mayor's office. Groundbreaking for Phase One of six phases was held.

Included in these six phases were: three runways, ramp area, service hangar, CAA annex, service shop, administration and airline offices, access roads, taxiways, beacon and runway lights. Also included was the transfer and remodeling of the Camp Grant Officers Ballroom for use as a terminal building.

This officers club building was adjacent to Airport Drive for a number of years.

In 1948 construction was begun on three 4,100-foot runways. These runways were built in the mode of the day: a triangle with the runways crossing each other to save land area. The idea was to have a runway that was always with the wind direction. These runways were 100' wide and made of 9" thick reinforced concrete. This aerial photo, shot in 1951, shows the distinctive runway pattern.

Another one of the original buildings that survived for quite a few years.

The Officers Ballroom building just before its move.

In 1950 the FAA flight service station was moved to the new airport from Machesney Field. This was the beginning of the end for Machesney as Rockford's major airport and it closed in 1974. This same year Charles W. Scott became the first General Manager of RFD. Warren Weaver, who had been Acting Manager, remained as Operations Chief.

During this time the Airport Authority, besides taking care of regular airport operations, also offered fuel sales and even ran the restaurant. Soon many of these services would be leased out. Fixed base operators (FBO's) would handle

Drive-up visitors were greeted with a propeller and anti-aircraft gun.

The Officers Ballroom building on the move to its new site.

The interior of the terminal building was 1950's modern, but was quite dated by the time it was replaced in 1987.

Airplane visitors were greeted by a very simple sign.

transient aviation services and other services would be leased to appropriate operations.

In 1952 the former Camp Grant Officers Ballroom (one of the 14 buildings included in the original deal) was moved to the new terminal site and extensively remodeled, including a brick exterior to give it a more substantial look. This old building served as the terminal until 1987.

The terminal building included ticket counters, baggage handling, security on the lower level and a restaurant, future bar and meeting room area on the upper. There was a three year fight with the city and county to receive a liquor license, and finally in 1960 the bar was opened. The food was good and the bar was cozy. We spent a few Friday nights at the airport enjoying the food, atmosphere and occasionally an airplane.

Most of the first six phases of construction were complete by 1953 and dedication was scheduled for November 1, 1954. This sunny, but chilly day attracted 15,000 visitors and included a tour of the airport along with a static aircraft display. This year Charles Scott resigned as General Manager of RFD and Grant Baer was appointed to the job.

Illinois Governor William Stratton made the formal dedication.

Both United and American Airlines had their latest cargo
versions of a DC-6 at the dedication, but it would take one of them almost 40
years before they brought passenger service to Rockford.

This 1952 aerial view gives an idea of the
airport at the time of the dedication.

In 1955 Grant Baer abruptly resigned and Robert Selfridge was appointed as General Manager. Warren Weaver also resigned and his duties were assigned to Selfridge.

Giving up on one of its FBO services, the GRAA leased all aircraft repairs to the newly formed Illini Airlines. Also in this year the Authority decided to handle snow removal that up to that time had been done by an outside firm. Greenlee Tool and

Robert Selfridge

Ingersoll Milling Machine leased maintenance hangar #1 for their DC-3 aircraft. They were the first corporate tenants.

The next year saw the construction of another larger maintenance hangar. This hangar could handle six DC-3s at one time and was leased to Illini for their repair services.

Twenty-eight thousand passengers enplaned at Rockford in 1956, a record at that time. The north/south runway (18-36) was extended by 700 ft. in 1957. Illini moved into its new home, maintenance hangar #2, and Butler Aviation moved its Beechcraft sales office into the small hangar vacated by Illini.

1958 saw Ozark board its 100,000 Rockford passenger and have its best year of travel in Rockford. Illini Airlines filed bankruptcy and gave up its lease to hangar #2. Ozark picked up the lease to use the hangar as its new northern headquarters. There were two new FBOs added: Northern Illinois Aviation Company, handling flight training and Business Air Transport that offered charter flights.

New maintenance hangar #2. This was to be the largest hangar built at RFD and is now occupied by Emery Air, Inc.

There was a far out proposal to build a civic auditorium in the Bell Bowl at the south end of the airport. Can you imagine how soundproof it would have had to be? Avis Rental proposed a motel on several acres of airport land. Nothing came of these proposals, but a proposal for industrial development was successful. The control tower became operational this year and plans were made to extend the north/south runway to 6,000 ft. and install an Instrument Landing System (ILS) for this runway. Robert Selfridge let the community know that in 1958 it costs $50.00 per hour to run the airport.

The Experimental Aircraft Association (EAA) brought its 1959 Convention to Rockford. Total attendance was 35,000, both spectators and conventioneers. Seventy homebuilt and antique aircraft were here and about 400 commercially built were flown in. The control tower reported 3,989 take offs and landings during the convention. The EAA convention had tremendous growth until its last convention in Rockford in 1970.

This 1961 photo shows the fledgling EAA convention. It was first held on the north side of the airport and later was moved to the southwest side.

The control tower was built in 1958 at a cost of $170,000 with the airport and CAA splitting the cost. Opening was scheduled for June 6 of that year, but was delayed until Oct. 11 due to lack of personnel to man it. The tower was sold to the FAA in 1969 and the FAA agreed to pay a $1.00 per year lease to the GRAA. There was some problem with moisture in the walls, but this was solved and the tower was recognized as one of the better-built at the time.

From the begining, there was not enough room in the tower. This addition to the north side of the tower was constructed in 1968.

This 1960 photo shows the equipment used at that time and the use of a hand-held beacon to signal aircraft.

Maintenance Hangar #2

Maintenance Hangar #1

Old Terminal B

This 1961 photo taken during the second EAA Convention shows the size of the airport at the time.

Original Hangar

Flight Service Building

T hangars (future site of UPS)

In 1960 the north/south runway extension was completed. The runway was now 4,800 feet long. As aircraft got bigger, the airport continually lengthened its runways. Ira Hartzog took over the Beechcraft dealership from Butler Aviation which was in maintenance hangar #1. EAA attendance reached 40,000, with 150 experimental aircraft and 1,000 commercially built aircraft.

Hartzog first occupied the original hangar next to the administration building and flight service center. These two photos from the 60s and 80s show the old hangar.

Originally built in 1955 for occupancy by Ingersoll Machine Tool and Greenlee Tool Company, this blue hangar (maintenance hangar #1) could hold Ingersoll's DC-3 and Greenlee's Viscount.

Ozark began service to O'Hare from Rockford in 1961. This year the ILS was to be put in service in March, but a problem arose. The old water tower northeast of the runway was causing problems and was interfering with the signal. This was the same water tower that was built in 1917 for the original Camp Grant. The tower was taken down and sold to the city of Rockford allowing the ILS to go operational in November.

The approach lights at the south end of runway 18-36 are shown in this 1960 photo. These lights aid in all approaches, including the ILS system.

In 1962 the Government removed the reverter clause in the GRAA deed. The clause said that in case of a national emergency, the land would revert back to the U.S. Government. This clause had limited growth and land leases up to that time. With the clause removed, Woodward Governor and Barber-Colman both leased airport land for corporate hangars.

The EAA Convention continued to grow, with 15,098 tower operations and over 200 aircraft. In 1963 the administration offices were moved to the weather station building.

This early 60's shot shows the original hangar occupied by Hartzog Aviation. Note the difference in the hanger door and roof. The hangar roof was raised later and a new door was added.

This year Ozark closed its Rockford Maintenance Facility, moving it to St. Louis. Hartzog moved into the vacated hangar #2. At this point, Hartzog occupied both hangars 1 and 2, and the original hangar near the weather service building.

Because of the EAA convention, on August 6, 1964 Rockford was the worlds busiest airport with 1,741 operations, as compared to O'Hare's 1,414.

In 1965 Runway 18-36 was extended to 6,000 feet... runway 7-25 to 5,000 feet. Ozark had 9 flights daily, but only 15 passengers per day. Business was declining...in 1957 there were 28,161 passengers but in 1964, only 7,109. Hartzog Aviation merged with Schneck Aviation this year.

EAA attendance was over 500,000 in 1966. 3,900 EAA members attended that year, with 6,000 commercially built aircraft and 389 homebuilt planes. There were 25,000 operations, but it was beginning to tax the airport's resources with 1,326 man-hours put in by airport staff.

In 1967 the new fire station on Falcon Rd. was completed and manned by Rockford Fire Dept. (Rockford station no. 7) The EAA had 32,024 take offs

and landings during its five-day show.

1970 saw the last EAA fly-in at Rockford, and the Association moved to Oshkosh, Wisconsin for 1971. There was much discussion on how this was handled at the time. The EAA annual convention went on to become one of the largest air attractions in the world. And there was always that "what if?" question. This year the GRAA Board appealed to the CAB for hyphenation with Chicago. This would allow airlines to serve RFD without CAB approval

Because of the new jumbo jets such as the 747 and DC-10, runway 18-36 was extended to 8,200 feet in 1971. The majority of the remaining Camp Grant buildings were demolished in 1974, and in 1976 there was considerable debate on $47 million Airport expansion.

A handsome biplane at the 1969 EAA Convention.

Robert Selfridge retired in 1977 and Bill Grady was named as new director. The first radar was installed at the airport this year.

In May of 1978 the $47 million expansion plan was finally approved. In 1979, upon a request from the GRAA board, the CAB declared Rockford a hyphenating point with Chicago. This allowed carriers who were serving Chicago to serve Rockford as they saw fit without CAB approval. Bill Grady retired in 1988 and Fred Ford became General Manager.

In 1991 the Airport was annexed to the city. Also, there was talk about building a golf course on airport property. It was finally decided that golf balls should not be flying at the airport.

The EAA Convention had grown and moved to the south side of the airport in 1964.

In 1994 Fred Ford resigned. James Loomis was appointed general manager.

A Modern New Terminal

Part of the 1978 plan was construction of a new terminal building. Construction was begun on the terminal in 1986 and it was opened in 1987. The cost was $4.9 million, which was part of a $5,234 million bond issue. This was the airport's only debt at the time.

The new terminal was built in front of the existing building. This allowed for more ramp space and the use of the old terminal building while the new one was being constructed.

The design, by Larson-Darby Architects, was open and airy and it has held up well, even by today's standards. Some changes have been made over the years but, the terminal has served as Rockford's front door to air travelers very effectively.

The steel skeleton begins to take the shape of the new building.

With the new terminal building and jetway almost completed, the old building is ready for the wrecking ball. This area was made into additional ramp area.

All that was left of the old terminal was a pile of rubble. After this was cleared off, the new ramp area was poured.

The ornate antique bar in St. James Envoy stood in contrast to the modern terminal.

In 1988 St. James Envoy restaurant was opened. This "fine dining" restaurant on the second floor of the terminal building was a real draw for local diners. In 2005 two new Jetways were added along with an improved baggage handling system. The new jetways gave RFD three arrival and departure gates and the new arrival lounge occupied the space formerly occupied by the restaurant.

This photo, taken just after the terminal was constructed, shows the main ticket counter area. The restaurant and jetway gate were upstairs.

Escalators were planned for on each side of the stairway...

...they were finally installed in 2007.

RFD Airline Service

In 1950 Mid-Continent Airlines began regular commercial service from Rockford to Chicago. This service was to Midway Airport utilizing DC-3s. In 1952 Mid-Continent merged with Braniff. At the time of the merger, Mid-Continent was operating a fleet of 23 Douglas DC-3's and four Convair 240's over its 6,241 miles of routes.

Braniff initially continued the operations from Greater Rockford, but finally discontinued its service in 1955. This was just the beginning of Rockford's turbulent association with many airlines.

In order to understand Rockford's relationship with passenger airline service, we need to take a look at the regulatory agency involved in the early years.

The Civil Aeronautics Board was formed in 1940 to handle safety, rule-making, accident investigation, and economic regulation of the airlines. The CAB regulated airfares and decided how many and which airlines could fly between cities. The Board regulated the number of flights during a given time period and the airline capacity, or the number of seats available.

The CAB said that new airlines needed to obtain a "certificate of public convenience and necessity" before offering flights between particular cities. The Board used these certificates as a way of regulating the number of competing airlines, issuing more certificates in good economic times and fewer in slow economic times or when fuel costs were high. Existing airlines also needed CAB approval to serve any new locale, and they could not eliminate service without CAB permission. Further, airlines needed approval to combine with other companies and to buy other companies.

The Airline Deregulation Act of 1978 phased out CAB's economic regulation of the airlines, and CAB ceased to exist at the end of 1984. So service to Rockford up until 1978 was severely regulated. Some airlines were serving Rockford because of CAB rules and not necessarily for economic gain. And, on the reverse side, some airlines could not serve Rockford because of these rules.

DC-3's were the main aircraft used by airlines after the war and during the 50's. Many were converted from the C-47, the Air force transport version of the DC-3.

AIRLINE TIMELINE

1950	Mid Continent
1951	Ozark
1952	Braniff
1955	Illini
1959	North Central
1967	Commuter
1972	Midstates
1978	Coleman
1980	TWA
1982	Mississippi Valley
1984	American Central
1984	Frontier
1986	Northwest Airlink
1989	Skyway
1989	Midway Connection
1990	American Eagle
1993	America West
2003	Trans Meridian
2004	Hooters Air
2005	Sunship 1
2005	Allegiant Airlines
2005	Northwest Airlink
2006	United Express

From 1950 to 1957 Rockford's air travel competition was Midway Airport in Chicago and Dane County airport in Madison. O'Hare opened in 1955 and didn't become a real competitor until 1962. Even though Midway was almost a three hour drive and Madison two hours, Rockford was having a hard time attracting passengers on a regular basis.

In 1962 Peoria-Rockford Bus company began furnishing service to O'Hare. With this new service, O'Hare was only one hour away by bus and any air service from Rockford was severely affected.

It seemed from this point on almost all flights from Rockford were based on connecting flights and were sold as such. The idea was to get travelers to use Greater Rockford Airport (RFD) to either avoid O'Hare or use RFD to fly to a connecting destination. As O'Hare grew it slowly sucked the air out of our struggling airport. As we will see, later on, this growth of O'Hare and it's congestion, size and expensive parking became a plus for RFD.

Ozark Airlines, Rockford's longest serving airline, offered service at various times from 1951 to 1982 flying to St. Louis, Omaha, Washington DC, Chicago, Moline, Waterloo, Iowa, and Denver. Ozark flew many different types of aircraft in many types of livery during this time, starting with the venerable DC-3 and including the Fairchild F27, Convair 240-4, Martin 404 and the DC-9.

Fairchild F27

Convair 240-4

Martin 404

DC-9

On the "down" side, in 1957 Ozark dropped four of their flights from Rockford. These were flights to Sioux City, Fort Dodge, Moline/Davenport/Rock Island and Minneapolis.

On the "up" side, in June of 1958 Ozark boarded its 100,000th passenger since beginning service in Rockford. At this time Ozark was offering service to St. Louis as well as other Midwest locations.

In 1959 Ozark leased maintenance hangar #2 for its Northern Headquarters and maintenance on its DC-3 fleet. Ozark also added flights to Omaha this year.

1961 saw Ozark offer service to the fast-growing O'Hare airport. But, the next year the Peoria-Rockford bus began their service to O'Hare with the bus fare being only $5.00. It was now only an hour to O'Hare by bus or car and our airlines were constantly fighting this competition.

In 1961, after only two years, Ozark closed its Rockford maintenance facility and moved out of the larger maintenance hangar. This was due to Ozarks headquarters move to St. Louis and the retirement of much of its DC-3 fleet.

In 1965 Ozark had nine flights from Rockford, but only 15 passengers per day. Business was declining rapidly. In 1957 there were 28,161 total passengers, in 1964 only 7,109. Rockford was beginning to really feel the effect of O'Hare. In 1966 Ozark cut three of these flights.

The relationship with Ozark was deteriorating in 1972 as the Airport board appealed to the CAB to oust Ozark because they were planning on dropping two more flights. There was trouble again in 1973 as Ozark flights were interrupted for three months with a strike.

In May 1976 Ozark began flights to Denver on a twice-daily basis. The airline kept expressing its satisfaction with the growth of passengers but was concerned with the number per flight. These flights originated at O'Hare. In May of 1976 there were 716 Rockford boardings and in August of that year there were 1,158. (The number of passengers per flight was only 18).

Strikes again affected Ozark in 1979 and 1980. These interruptions severely affected passenger loyalty and in 1982 Ozark quit Rockford for good. In the 21 years that Ozark served Rockford there were many ups and downs. Both Ozark and the Airport tried to make the relationship work on a profitable basis. The CAB, O'Hare and work interruptions all contributed to its leaving Rockford.

As one of Rockford's longest-serving airlines, Ozark won the respect of many local travelers. These photos of a restored Ozark DC-3 may bring back memories for many of these people.

In 1955 Illini Airlines, a small commuter line, began service from Rockford to Meigs Field in Chicago. (The downtown lakeshore airport was shut down by the City of Chicago in 2001.) Illini's home base was Rockford, utilizing maintenance

hangar #2. They flew gangly looking De Havilland Dove aircraft, shown on the right. Due to a number of circumstances Illini went bankrupt in 1960.

North Central began flights from Rockford to Madison and Chicago in 1959. Again these flights were short-lived... with the new I-90 driving was too easy. The service ended in 1960.

Midwest Commuter Airlines decided to furnish flights from Rockford to both Chicago O'Hare and Meigs Field. This service lasted from 1967 to 1969.

This seemed to be the beginning of airlines serving Rockford for two to three years before suspending service. The Rockford market was still difficult because of the rise of O'Hare and the convenience of bus transportation to that airport. Quite often the airlines that tried to serve Rockford went out of business or were merged with larger airlines.

Fly **ILLINI** AIRLINES

America's Friendliest Airline
NOW OFFERS
Golden Age Liner Service
To
MADISON, WIS. -ROCKFO
FREEPORT
STERLING-ROCK FALLS
And
DOWNTOWN CHICAG
MEIGS FIELD
EFFECTIVE NOVEMBER 1, 1953
F L I G H T S   D A I L
Illini Airlines, Inc.

ILLINI AIRLINES

**Route of the Golden Arrows serving
ROCKFORD, MADISON, FREEPORT,
STERLING-ROCK FALLS...AND
DOWNTOWN CHICAGO**
(Meigs Field)

**MIDWEST
COMMUTER
AIRLINES**
TIME TABLE EFFECTIVE JULY 1, 1967

FLY
TODAY
WITH
MCA

YOUR DOWNTOWN AIRLINE

TH CENTRAL. N2041

Convair 580

61

But they wouldn't give up trying. 1978 saw the beginning of Coleman Airlines. Founded by Phillip Coleman, Coleman Air Transport was based out of Rockford, Illinois. Mr. Colman was a distributor for Beech Aircraft Corporation and earned numerous sales awards selling the popular King Air series aircraft.

Coleman Air Transport offered scheduled service throughout the Midwest and was also a provider of aircraft to the United States government for diplomatic and intelligence operations. Colman Air

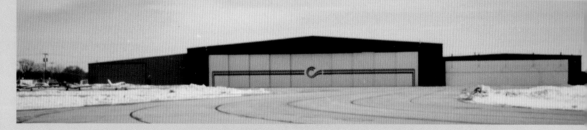

Transport offered flights to Detroit and Minneapolis until 1980. Trying for too fast a growth, Coleman soon got in financial and FAA regulation trouble and went out of business. During their short heyday Coleman built the large hangar on the east side of the airport and even had a DC-9 ready for service. The hangar reverted back to the airport when Coleman went bankrupt.

The first major airline to serve Rockford was TWA. TWA offered service to O'Hare from 1980 to 1982. TWA offered jet service using Boeing 727's. As an international airline TWA promoted the fact that you could reach many cities in Europe from Rockford.

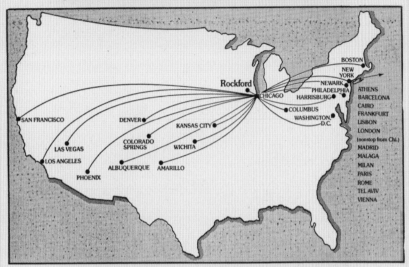

AIRLINE TIMELINE

1950	Mid Continent
1951	Ozark
1952	Braniff
1955	Illini
1959	North Central
1967	Commuter
1972	Midstates
1978	Coleman
1980	TWA
1982	Mississippi Valley
1984	American Central
1984	Frontier
1986	Northwest Airlink
1989	Skyway
1989	Midway Connection
1990	American Eagle
1993	America West
2003	Trans Meridian
2004	Hooters Air
2005	Sunship 1
2005	Allegiant Airlines
2005	Northwest Airlink
2006	United Express

MVA
FLIGHT SCHEDULE

NEW Service Between Waterloo/Cedar Falls and Chicago. Added service from Milwaukee to Chicago.

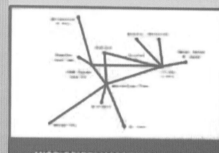

MISSISSIPPI VALLEY AIRLINES

AMERICAN CENTRAL AIRLINES

Systems Timetable
Effective November 1, 1984

ANNOUNCING NEW LOCATION
at
CHICAGO O'HARE

Ticket Counter - Terminal 3
U.S. AIR
Boarding Gate — G 5
Reservations & Air Freight
In Iowa............(800) 942-9000
Elsewhere..........(800) 553-9000
or (319) 236-9010

N7341F

FRON

After TWA suspended service, Mississippi Valley Airlines picked up the flights to O'Hare from 1982 to 1984. Mississippi Valley merged with Air Wisconsin in 1985.

American Central Airlines, formerly Mid-Continent Airlines (the second airline with that name) had service from Rockford to Detroit in 1984 and 1985.

In 1984 Frontier Airlines, flying Boeing 737's, offered service to Denver with connecting flights to other destinations in the West. Frontier crews over-nighted in Rockford and the early morning flight left about 6:00 am. This was far from a non-stop flight. From Rockford the first stop was Cedar Rapids, Iowa; next: Des Moines, then Denver. If you liked take-offs and landings it was great. If you didn't, then you probably flew from Chicago.

The return flight went to Madison then Rockford. On the few flights that I took on Frontier, it was just the crew and myself when we landed in Rockford. This service lasted from 1984 to 1986 (again a service lasting two years). Frontier went bankrupt in 1986.

Northwest Airlines has its own code sharing network of regional airlines operating as Northwest Airlink. Northwest began service to Detroit and Minneapolis from Greater Rockford Airport in 1986. This service lasted until 2001. Northwest Airlink returned to Rockford in 2005 with service to Detroit, but this service didn't last long and ended after about six months. The fare to the initial destination, Detroit, was not competitive with Northwest's fare from O'Hare. So it was much less money to fly out of O'Hare even with the extra bus cost or parking fees.

The BAE Jetstream 31 was one type of aircraft that Northwest flew to Rockford.

Skyway flew Beech 19 airliners to Milwaukee and Detroit.

Major airlines furnishing flights from Rockford, using their commuter partners, based their rates on getting the connecting business and many times were not interested in selling the initial destination or competing with their O'Hare fares.

Skyway Airlines flew from Rockford to Milwaukee and Detroit from 1989 to 1997. Also known as Midwest Connect, Midwest Airlines, Skyway Airlines and The Midwest Express Connection, it began flight operations on April 17, 1989 in Milwaukee. Astral Aviation was formed in 1994, and began Skyway operations in February of that year. The airline simplified its name to Midwest Connect in March 2003. Even with the name confusion, Skyway served Rockford for eight years.

One of the larger aircraft Northwest Airlink flew at the time was the SAAB 340B.

AIRLINE TIMELINE

May 1989 ad for Midway Airlines. This offer was in conjunction with a local bank and sold the idea of low fares.

Skyway took the high road and stressed comfort and extras.

Midway Connection flew from Rockford to Midway Airport for connecting flights on Midway Airlines. The airline began seven round trips per day in 1988, using Dornier 228 Turbo Props and ended service in 1990.

AIRLINE TIMELINE

1950	Mid Continent
1951	Ozark
1952	Braniff
1955	Illini
1959	North Central
1967	Commuter
1972	Midstates
1978	Coleman
1980	TWA
1982	Mississippi Valley
1984	American Central
1984	Frontier
1986	Northwest Airlink
1989	Skyway
1989	Midway Connection
1990	American Eagle
1993	America West
2003	Trans Meridian
2004	Hooters Air
2005	Sunship 1
2005	Allegiant Airlines
2005	Northwest Airlink
2006	United Express

American Eagle, a regional airline partner of American Airlines, furnished two flights daily to Chicago O'Hare from 1990-96. These flights were connecting flights with connections to all of American's destinations from Chicago. In a way they were competing with the Peoria-Rockford bus runs to O'Hare. These flights, if part of an American Airlines connecting flight from Chicago, were basically free. In fact, competitor United Airlines offered free bus fare to O'Hare and back on Peoria-Rockford's runs to fight these American fares. United ended this free bus fare in 2002.

"From boondoggle to boon" the headline in the April 23, 1990 Rockford Register Star suggested that RFD had finally turned the corner for airline service. Four airlines were serving the city, handling over 7,000 passengers a month, yet 10 years later all were gone.

With American Eagle flights ending in 1996 and Northwest Airlink's last flight in 2001, Rockford was without passenger service for the first time since 1950.

This 1985 aerial view shows the lengthened 18-26 runway. With its new length of 8,200 ft. it could now handle the larger jumbo jets such as the Boeing 747. The old terminal building is still in place, but soon to be replaced.

Operations

From snow removal to fire protection and security, an airport is like a small city. In 1955 the GRAA decided to handle their own snow removal, that up to that time had been contracted to an outside firm. Because the airport was well known for its expertise in snow removal and emergency services it was often used for emergencies and weather-related landings.

Maintenance and other operations were originally housed on the east side of the airport on Falcon Drive. When Schneck Aviation left their hangar and facility south of the terminal, the hangar was remodeled to house the fire and security equipment. This later became the International Gate, and the rest of the facility now houses the GRAA administrative offices. In 1991 the operation of the airports fire-fighting equipment was turned over to the Rockford Fire Department and an addition was made to the existing fire station on Falcon Road to house the vehicles. Then, in 2004, the snow removal and security equipment were moved to the new maintenance facility built just south of the tower.

Airport maintenance was originally housed in this facility on the east side of the airport now housing the Charter Coach Company.

This addition was added on to the ramp side of Rockford Fire Station 7 to house the airport equipment.

Emergency vehicle "Charlie" circa 1960.

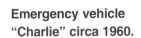

Emergency vehicle "Baker" circa 1960.

Fire in building six being fought by the RFD firefighters. The fire took place in 1956.

On July 15, 1961 a U.S. Navy R5D made an emergency landing at RFD after having a warning light on its #2 engine.

The administration has always made use of existing structures at the airport to house its operations. They used existing Camp Grant buildings at first, then moved from the old weather station building to a building on Kishwaukee Rd. now occupied by UPS. From there, they moved to the present location. in the old Schneck building. The sign in front of the old Camp Grant building above says Greater Rockford Airport Engineer.

The administration offices were in this building for a short time.

With bad weather at O'Hare Rockford became a safe haven in this 1998 photo.

The weather station building shown in this photo, taken around 1960, housed the airport administration offices for a short time. The building was torn down in 1980. Notice the Hartzog sign... advertising the fact that they were an FBO.

The old Schneck building hangar was remodeled to house the fire and security equipment and personnel in 1985.

The airport fire protection services consisted of three main pieces of equipment. The larger vehicles shown were known as "Chubs." There was constant training and rehearsals for possible accidents and fires.

From the day the airport opened, snow removal has always been a priority. In fact, over the years the airport has only been shut down once because of snow, and that was just for a matter of hours.

One of the biggest tasks for the snow removal crew is keeping the runways open all through the night for UPS.

This photo from 1969 shows how well equipped the airport snow removal crews were at that time.

The new 40,000 sq. ft. maintenance facility opened in 2005.

Integrated Airport Services

An integral part of any airport operations, but not as high a public profile as airline service, are the other aircraft related business. These include Fixed Base Operators (FBO's), corporate aircraft hangars, aircraft charter operations, aircraft sales companies, cargo operators, aircraft maintenance and restoration. RFD also has an educational facility... Rock Valley College.

An FBO offers fueling and other ramp services for corporate or private aircraft using the airport. They would be similar to a service station on a freeway, except with more services for pilots and passengers.

This photo from the 50's shows Hartzog in the south hangar next to the weather service building.

Maintenance hangar #1 occupied by Hartzog Aviation. It was torn down in 1988 for more ramp space.

Over the years there have been many FBO's and other aircraft related businesses with ramp access at RFD. In 1957, with the completion of maintenance hangar #2, the GRAA had three hangars available for lease. Illini Aviation occupied #2, Butler Aviation moved its Beechcraft sales office into maintenance hangar #1 that was vacated by Illini, and Hartzog was in the original hangar south of the terminal.

Maintenance hangar No. 2 when occupied by Hartzog Aviation. Over the years this hangar also has been home to Illini Airlines, Ozark Airlines and now Emery Air, Inc. The large Beechcraft logo can still be seen on the south end of the building.

Schneck Aviation built this hangar and rebuilding facility in 1969. The building eventually housed the airport administration offices and International Terminal.

Built in 1984 by Alpine Aviation, now owned by Kaney Aerospace.

This hangar is now owned by Kaney Aerospace.

First occupied by TDM, this hangar now houses Heritage Aviation.

This hangar was home to Atwood and now houses RD Air.

Built in 1980 by Sundstrand, this hangar is now home to RD Air.

This classic looking hangar was built by Barber Colman and is now owned by Kaney Aerospace Aviation services.

Built in 1957 by the Airport, this hangar now houses Emery Air.

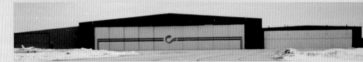

Built in 1957 by Coleman Air, this hangar now houses Emery Air RJ maintenance and Emery Automotive Services.

Built by Sundstrand, this hangar was purchased by Courtesy Aircraft in 1980 and is still occupied by Courtesy.

Built in the 70's, this hangar was home to D&E Aviation, Rockford Acromatic.

This hangar and manufacturing building was built by Schneck Aviation. It is now the International Terminal and administration building.

This hangar was home to Hydro Line and is now used by the airport.

This hangar was built by Aero Taxi in 1980. It was home to Newell, and now houses North American Aviation.

This hangar was also built by Aero Taxi in 1980 and now houses Pride Aircraft.

Who's Who and Who's Where.

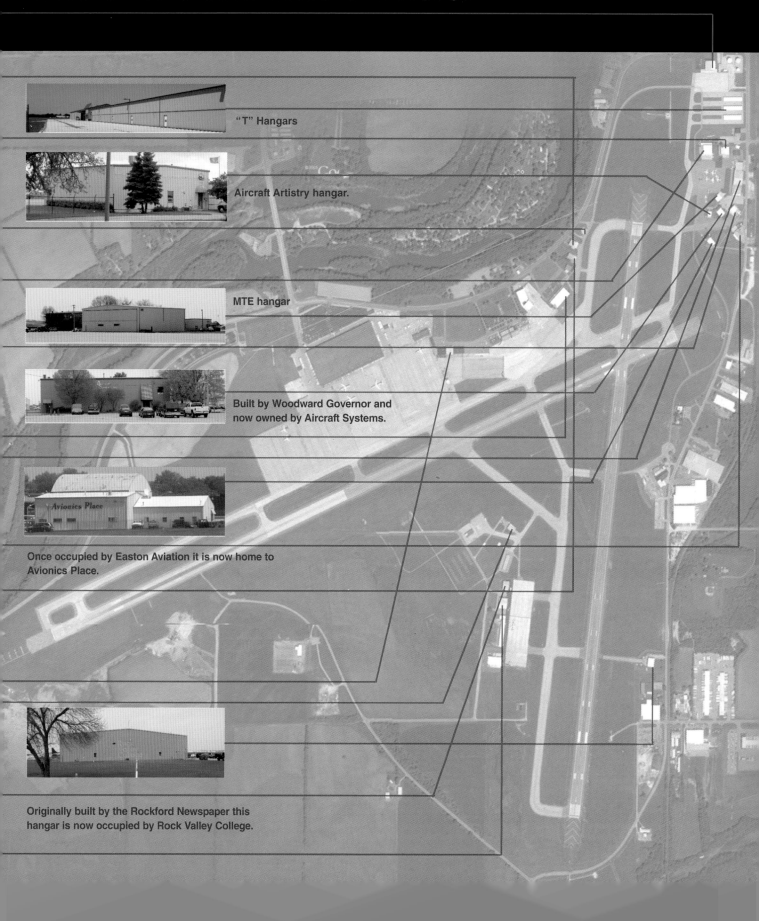

"T" Hangars

Aircraft Artistry hangar.

MTE hangar

Built by Woodward Governor and now owned by Aircraft Systems.

Avionics Place

Once occupied by Easton Aviation it is now home to Avionics Place.

Originally built by the Rockford Newspaper this hangar is now occupied by Rock Valley College.

Kaney Aerospace

Kaney Aerospace is now in this 20,400 square foot hangar built by Alpine Aviation in 1984. Alpine handled aircraft maintenance and offered charter flights. Alpine is now in a smaller facility on Falcon Road.

Skyways Airlines moved into the hangar in 1991 and left soon after. Pioneer Life Insurance had their corporate aircraft in the hangar for a few years, and Newell Company moved their corporate aviation facilities from the south apron to this hangar before Kaney Jet Aerospace took over the hangar in 2005.

Kaney offers testing and evaluation of aircraft components, system integrations and assembly and light manufacturing. For extreme temperature testing, Kaney has one of the largest thermal chambers in the Midwest.

That tail you see sticking out of the Kaney hangar is a 737-200.

The Kaney Aerospace thermal chamber is located in the corner of the hangar for easy access.

The 737-200 is part of a joint venture with Kaney Aerospace and Matrix. The aircraft is used to test emerging wireless technologies.

Heritage Aero, Inc.

Heritage Aero, Inc. now occupies the hangar built in 1980 by TDM Harwood. Heritage offers quality maintenance services for military aircraft and maintenance services for a wide variety of civilian general aviation aircraft. Heritage Aero also specializes in disassembling and crating aircraft for shipment worldwide.

T-28 with cowling off for maintenance.

Alpine Aviation Corp.

Alpine Aviation is now housed in this facility on 5015 Falcon Road. Alpine offers charter service and also life vest and life raft certifications. An A/P is on hand for aircraft maintenance.

Courtesy Aircraft

In 1957 D.M. "Swede" Clark founded Courtesy Aircraft, Inc. one of RFD's longest tenants. Mr. Clark was well known in the Rockford area for his auto dealerships. Through the 60's Courtesy sales included new Cessna, Piper and Champion aircraft. Courtesy was also very active in the used airplane market. In fact, one of the first-ever airplane auctions was held by Courtesy in 1957. In the early 70's Mark Clark, Swedes son, became an accomplished

Since Swede was also in the auto sales business, it made sense that he would provide a "courtesy" car for his airport clients.

Part of the turnout for the 1957 auction.

The hangar as it is today.

pilot and A&P mechanic and found a new market in selling Warbirds. Most of these were of World War II and Korean War era.

In the early 80's Mark purchased the company from his father and relocated in a 13,000 sq. ft. hangar on the east side of the airport. This hangar was vacated by Sundstrand when they moved to a new hangar across the apron. With over 3,000 aircraft sold and delivered, Courtesy Aircraft and its international reputation is a real plus for RFD.

Swede and Mark, father and son - one of Rockford's aircraft legacies.

This beautifully restored P51 Mustang is just one of the many aircraft to occupy the Courtesy Hangar.

In 1958 there were two new FBO's: Northern Illinois Aviation Company, handling flight training, and Business Air Transport, offering charter flights. They both were located in the "T" hangars south of the terminal building. Northern Illinois offered flight training, while BAT was offering charter flights using the De Havilland Dove that was flown by Illini Airlines, now defunct, .

Hartzog Aviation

When his employer, Butler Aviation gave up its Beech franchise at RFD in 1960, Ira Hartzog decided to take it. He at first just sold Beech Aircraft, but little by little he expanded into flight-line services and other maintenance services. He also added a flight department with charter pilots and flight instructors.

WHEN YOU WANT ANSWERS TO YOUR QUESTIONS ABOUT:

• Aircraft Charter
• Aircraft Rental
• Primary and Advanced Flight Training
• New & Used Beechcraft Sales
• Aircraft Service and Repair

CALL US, WE'RE HARTZOG AVIATION

and we've been answering your questions about flying for 21 years.

987-4100

HARTZOG AVIATION
The Midwest's largest Beechcraft Corporate Center
Greater Rockford Airport • P.O. Box 6107 • Rockford, Illinois 61125

In 1962 Hartzog moved into the large maintenance hangar that had been occupied by Ozark. In 1965 Hartzog merged with Schneck aviation, an engine rebuilder. Hartzog was sold to Ratheon (the owner of Beechcraft) in 1985.

Hartzog occupying the large maintenance hangar in this photo from the early 60's.

The old blue hangar (maintenance hangar #1) was torn down in the mid 80's to make room for ramp space and the new Emery hangar.

Aero Taxi

Aero Taxi was begun by Rich Gibson in 1974,, and in 1980 he built the hangar now occupied by Pride Aircraft. Aero Taxi offered air charter and FBO services.

Rich now has Rich's Incredible Pyro. His company puts on pyrotechnics displays at airshows all over the world. If you been to any Rockford airshows you've seen Rich's spectacular work

CARGO PROBLEMS?
NEEDED IT YESTERDAY?
CUSTOMERS UPSET?

AERO TAXI
CAN HELP
U.S. GOVERNMENT CERTIFIED
AIRCRAFT CHARTER SERVICE
SERVING ROCKFORD, UNITED STATES, CANADA AND MEXICO

24-HR. SERVICE
963-4444 Richard E. Gibson, President
AERO TAXI – ROCKFORD, INC.
Greater Rockford Airport

Ground Handling Service Available with FREE Pick-up
and Delivery in Rockford area — Freight to your customers
in a matter of Hours — NOT Days

Avionics Place

Avionics Place was started in 1981 and offers T-28 upgrades and services, autopilot repair and service, avionics repair, and VFR & IFR Biennial FAR's Certifications.

Emery Air Inc.

In 1972 Lew Emery, Rockford Manufacturer and importer, built a new hangar near the terminal for his Emery Air Charter Service. Emery was managing his own airplanes and others used for charter purposes. In 1998 the Thomas family, owners of the Poplar Grove Airport north of Belvidere, Illinois, acquired Emery Air Charter. In 2003 the Thomas's created a diverse aircraft service company by acquiring Raytheon Aircraft Services, which operated out of the large maintenance hangar. Now known as Emery Air Inc., the company

opened a regional airline maintenance center, occupying the large east side hangar. This service includes everything from heavy maintenance to avionics repair on the popular Canadair family of RJ jets. Emery also has an FBO center and handles ramp services for UPS and other airlines serving Rockford.

An Emery A/P working on an RJ engine.

Emery also services land-based vehicles through Emery Automotive Services.

"T" Hangars

There are "T" hangars on the northeast side of the airport. The Airport Authority has hangars for rent and "condo" hangars are available from Moreland Enterprises.

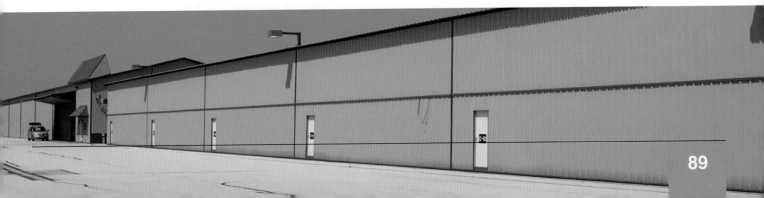

89

Pride Aircraft /North American Aviation

Pride Aircraft moved to its current location in 2003. This hangar was previously occupied by Heritage Aero. Pride was founded in 1989 by John Morgan and they initially restored T-28's. In 1996 they began restoring L-39's a jet fighter made for Russia by Aero Vodochody, a Czechoslovakian company. Pride also offers aircraft sales, avionics and L-39 flight training. North American Aviation is a full service FBO.

Mechanic at work on one of the L-39s.

D&E Aviation was formed in 1968 occupying the hangar that was vacated by Bruton Smith, a Rockford automobile dealer. Harold "IKE" Eicher, one of the founders, was specializing in air-

craft sales for Rockford area customers. He found a Beech Queen air for Rockford Acromatic Corp. and eventually leased the hangar to them and flew the aircraft. Ike retired in 2000 and Rockford Acromatic gave up the hangar that year.

Aircraft Systems

Founded by Terry Norris in 1970, Aircraft Systems, Inc specializes in the repairing, overhauling and troubleshooting of general aviation aircraft accessories. Aircraft Systems is located in the hangar previously owned by Woodward Governor Co. Aircraft Systems is well known throughout the corporate and civil aviation world.

Aircraft Artistry

Owner Del Wildes is a former USMC jet mechanic who has airbrushed for over 30 years. Besides adding their artistry to aircraft, they also do other types of vehicles.

Rock Valley College

This aerial photo from the early 70's shows the RVC hangar, the DC-3 donated by the Rockford Newspaper and the F-86 donated by the U.S. Airforce.

Rock Valley College has had a presence at RFD since 1970 and has been offering a A/P (Airframe/Powerplant) Certification course since 1968. This intensive training is necessary for any mechanic to work on any aircraft.

In 1970, the Rockford newspaper sold its hangar to the college and at the same time donated their corporate aircraft, a DC-3, to them for A/P training purposes.

Over the years, RVC has received many aircraft under different circumstances. The F-86 sabre jet shown below was given to the city by the Air Force. The city decided the best place for it was at Rock Valley rather than rusting away in some park.

A young Chuck Billman, now an RVC professor, working on one of the DC-3 engines in this early 70's photo.

This Aero Commander was a popular twin engine aircraft in the 60's and 70's. Its now available for A/P training.

A current class at RVC working on gear retraction and extension.

Air Cargo Services

Because of its centralized location and proximity to Chicago, RFD was a natural location for air cargo operations.

In the 1980s Federal Express was courted to open operations at the airport, but to no avail. In 1989 Emery Worldwide, an air cargo company , flew one of their aircraft into Rockford on a regular basis. With the amount of the automotive businesses in the area, the inbound freight was enough to attract Emery, but the outgoing cargo was not enough to sustain the service and it was short-lived.

Airbourne Express was the first to have a permanent presence at RFD. In 1991 they built a new 26,000 sq. ft. cargo handling facility on the south ramp and were soon acquired by DHL Global. DHL's distinctive yellow and red DC-9s can be seen daily at RFD.

In 1993 UPS announced they would build a major sorting facility at Greater Rockford Airport. This 500,000 sq. ft. facility was opened in 1994, and the positive effect for RFD was tremendous. Besides the centralized location, Rockford's operational record and up-to-date snow removal equipment played a large part in their decision to choose RFD. In 2001 BAX Global began operations at the airport becoming the airport's third cargo carrier.

Straight Shot Express located at the airport in 2004. As an express ground transporter, Straight Shot was a natural fit for RFD's air cargo operations.

DHL, BAX Global and Straight Shot are all located at the south ramp.

The familiar red and yellow DC-9 of DHL.

Runway 7-25... 10,004 feet long to handle the largest of the cargo fleet.

The UPS building and ramp under construction.
Note how the ramps 18" thick concrete pours
were done in alternating strips.

The UPS facility was constructed in 1994. The ramp area was twice as large as the building to handle up to 15 aircraft at one time. Also at this time the east west runway 7-25 was extended to 10,004 feet, making it among the longest in Illinois.

The runway 7-25 extension under construction. The UPS facility is on the right. The south ramp can be seen in the far left of this photo.

The Concorde, September 21, 1985

We could hear the pilot in his distinctive English accent asking for a low pass over 36, a teardrop and return over 18 for another low pass. The Concorde was arriving from New York with some Rockford dignitaries and was picking up a paying group for a return trip to London. After landing on runway 36, the craft taxied to the terminal building.

We were at, what was then, Easton Aviation across the airport on Falcon Drive. The EAA local chapter was sponsoring a pig roast for the crew of the Concorde... all 12 of them! Since this was an international flight with a stop in New York, they had to have two complete crews of six cockpit and six flight attendants.

I had decided to do a painting commemorating the event and have it ready when the Concorde arrived. The original painting was set up in the Easton Hangar and the entire crews signed the original. Limited edition prints were made and the original painting was sold to a couple from the Chicago area who had traveled on the flight.

It flies at twice the speed of sound.

The tickets will probably go even faster.

Only two flights to London on the Concorde SST Oct. 22 & Oct. 30
AAA Travel Agency.

Originally scheduled to land at O'Hare, the Concorde came to Rockford instead. O'Hare felt it would be too loud to land there. This ad promotes the fact that it was coming to "Illinois"... not Rockford... just Illinois.

One of the limited edition prints.

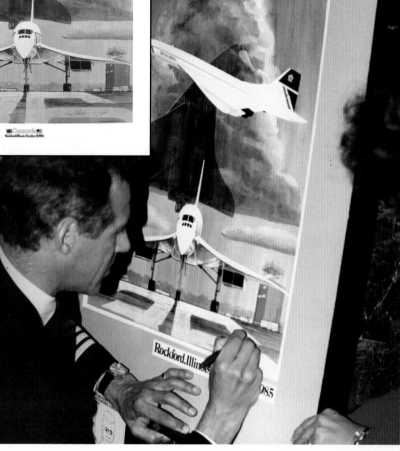

Captain Richard
Boras signing
the original painting.

The Concorde taxiing
up to the terminal.

RFD Air Shows and Special Events

The first airshow was the Bicentenial Show held at RFD in 1976 and featured the Air Force Thunderbirds.

The first Confederate Air Force Show was held in 1981. The show had a flying demonstration of a Japanese Zero and the B-17, "Texas Raiders" attracted its share of spectators. The CAF* show was held again in 1983.

The 1988 Show (Airshow/Rockford 88), July 16-17, again featured the Thunderbirds, along with Julie Clark and Bob Blankenship. The ticket prices were $5 and $8. Another B-17, "Sentimental Journey" was one of the main attractions.

The Confederate Air Force is now known as the Commemorative Air Force

The B-17 "Texas Raiders" is owned by the CAF (Commemorative Air Force) Gulf Coast Wing.

The B-17 "Sentimental Journey" is owned by the Arizona Wing of the CAF.

The Air Force static display at the 1989 show.

The 1989 show attracted 75,000 visitors and the Littlefields, a husband and wife team, were one of the performers.

In July, 1990, the airshow had Mig 29's and other Warbirds such as a B-17, T-28's and a P-51. Since the show was competing with the Chicago airshow, the attendance was only 35,000 on the first day.

In 1991 the Thunderbirds and Cheryl Rae and Gene Littlefield again appeared. The B-17 "Memphis Belle" was also on display.

Rockford Air Shows were organized independently of the airport from 1986 until the last show in 1996. Difficulty with attendance and sponsorships caused the organization that put on the shows to disband, and there were no more shows held until 2005. It was decided that year that the GRAA would conduct the shows. Rockford AirFests are now held under the auspices of the Greater Rockford Airport Authority.

These air shows are heavily dependent on volunteers and local sponsorships. Over 1000 volunteers pitched in to make the 2007 air show a success.

Bonanza Fly-ins

Started in 1995, these spectacular fly-ins of up to 100 Beechcraft aircraft continue each year to this day. Always arriving in Rockford the weekend before the EAA Convention in Oshkosh, the American Bonanza Society fly-in is high "hangar" talk. The aircraft depart three abreast for the trip to Oshkosh.

"Cleared for take-off" as real meaning as the planes begin their take-off roll.

A classic "V" tail taxing to the active in the 2007 photo.

The pilots check-in tent from the 1997 fly-in.

Presidential Visits

Over the years, a few presidents and vice presidents have visited RFD. Vice President Richard Nixon was the first in 1956. In 1964 Lyndon Johnson made it a point to say that he was the first Democrat President to visit Rockford.

Richard Nixon returned as president in 1970 and in 1976 Gerald Ford and his wife, Betty, came to the airport. In 1984 President Reagan was here for 11 minutes before taking a helicopter to Dixon. I don't know what it says about Rockford, but it has been over 20 years since a U.S. president has set foot in our town.

Vice President George Bush and his wife Barbara arriving in Rockford on Air Force 2.

Gerald Ford's arrival in 1976. That's Betty Ford in the doorway. Not sure why they were traveling on a C-9, the military version of the DC-9.

President Nixon's arrival in 1970. It's a good shot of the plane and crowd, and we're sure Nixon is in there somewhere.

AIRFEST/05/06

(top) Courtesy Aircraft's classic DC-3 and a T-38 trainer were part of the 2005 static display.

(center) Ryan Airlines 757 seems to be keeping a watch on the crowd.

Dave Dacy and his flag-carrying wing walker.

Not really "Hard to Get" if you got enough money, this beautiful
A-26 invader was an attraction at the 2005 show.

AIRFEST/07

140,000 people!... a great turnout for Airfest/07, despite threatening weather. The big draw was the Navy Blue Angels flying their F-18 Hornets in tight four and six plane formations. A few weeks earlier the Angels had lost one of their own in an airshow in Beaufort, South Carolina.

After the show the Blue Angel pilots signed autographs for the fans and attracted quite a crowd. One of Rockford's own is a member of the Blue Angels support team. Drew Hess flies the C-130 known as Fat Albert.

P-51, F-16 and a F-15 in tight formation.

Dave Dacy, a perennial favorite.

The Red Baron Aerobatic team.

Clint Harris, Number 3, signs a Blue Angel T-shirt for my wife, Diane.

U.S. NAVY

A New Beginning

In 2001 James Loomis resigned, and in 2002 Bob O'Brien was named Airport Executive Director. Bob came to a well-equipped, modern airport with no scheduled passenger airline service. His first priority was to get a scheduled airline to come to RFD. In short order he found one... TransMeridian Airline (TMA), a small scheduled charter airline would come to Rockford if... the community would come up with $500,000 to market the airline's service out of Rockford. With the GRAA board's approval to provide $250,000 all Bob needed was an additional $250,000 from the citizens and businesses in the area!

Most people agreed that it sounded like an impossible task. O'Brien put his faith in the community and began a tireless PR campaign. He was on television, radio, newspaper and even on the roof of a gas station pleading with Rockford to come up with the money. Apparently he hit a nerve... the community did want the airport to succeed and were more than willing to "pay" up. By the time the tight deadline had arrived Bob had raised $269,687! He was over his goal, and TransMeridian was on its way to RFD.

In July 2003, Rob Binns, President of TMA, and a contingent flew up to Rockford for a welcoming ceremony. Binns was absolutely amazed at the turnout and support. "It's an incredible turnout. I was expecting maybe 100 people" was one of his many comments. There were over 2000 people to greet him. TMA's inaugural flight

was August 28, 2003 and Rockford was at last being serviced by a scheduled airline.

The well-known restaurant chain, Hooters, was getting into the airline business and decided to offer flights out of Rockford to Las Vegas, Atlanta, Denver and Myrtle Beach. Their inaugural flight was February 3, 2005.

Now we had two airlines serving Rockford... but not for long. TMA was a struggling charter airline using a limited number of older 727's and 757's. Although the service they were offering from Rockford to Las Vegas and Orlando, Florida was successful, they succumbed to lack of operating funds and declared bankruptcy in fall of 2005.

Hooters decided the airline business wasn't for them and they shut down their airline in the fall of 2005. It looked as though it was happening again... airline service for one or two years, then none.

The ceremony to welcome TMA was on a rainy July day, but it could not deter the 2,000 plus airport supporters from coming out to see the new airline.

This support and the fact that TMA's flights were successful as far as number of passengers was concerned, meant that Rockford had proven itself.

After TMA suspended service, Allegiant Airlines immediately saw the opportunity and began flights to Las Vegas on November 3, 2005. They soon offered flights to Orlando and Tampa/St. Petersburg.

The year 2005 also saw two other beginnings. Northwest decided to again offer service from Rockford to Detroit with connections throughout the world. Sunship, a new charter line, offered service to CanCun Mexico. With this service to Mexico, RFD was officially an International Airport.

Due to fares that were not competitive enough with flights from O'Hare, Northwest ended their Rockford flights in January 2006.

Sunship succumbed to other pressures and ended flights a year later. These flights did continue as regular charter flights through other charter operators.

During this time of a new beginning, the enthusiasm and excitement drove me to paint a commemorative picture of TMA's first flight from Rockford.

After showing it to the people at the airport and winning their approval, we decided to keep the enthusiasm going by doing a painting for each new airline flying out of Rockford.

These paintings now hang in the arrival/departure gate area.

United Express flies the
Canadair RJ500 to Denver.

It was finally time for United Airlines to come to Rockford in the form of United Express. (Remember that airport dedication photo from 1954?) The inaugural flight to Denver was on March 3, 2006 utilizing the popular Canadair Regional Jet. Ridership has been very good with many connections from Denver to destinations west.

United's fares have been competitive with O'Hare and the free parking and no hassle service from RFD is finally paying off. With the larger airports becoming more congested and with the new 50 and 70 seat Regional Jets (RJs), the trend is definitely towards the smaller airports such as RFD. On one trip to Denver on United we saw over 10 RJ's on the ramp ready to depart to destinations all over the U.S.

Allegiant, using 150 seat MD-80's, found the Las Vegas flights to be very popular and soon offered flights to Orlando, Tampa/St. Petersbur, Phoenix-Mesa, and Fort Lauderdale.

Allegiant is also leading the trend in serving the secondary airports. Their route map is, what I feel, a vision of the future... an airline serving many smaller cities with convenient on-time service, while avoiding the congested hubs.

With Rockford's ranking as an airport offering passenger service rising from 630 in 2000 to 224 today, Bob O'Brien is shooting to get RFD into the top 100 and with continued support from the community we should make it. RFD is now one on the top cargo airports in the country (ranking 21st).

Although we are still The Greater Rockford Airport, we are now known as Chicago Rockford International Airport. (CRFD) This gives the airport a name that is more recognizable throughout the world.

Allegiant's MD-80's are their most used aircraft.

If They Could See Us Now!

Ninety years since the ground breaking for
Camp Grant. The changes and the progress
has been tremendous. In fact, in 2007 we
were named Illinois Primary Airport of the Year

That old saying, "The only constant is change"
makes me wonder what the next 90 years will bring.

Will we become as big as O'Hare?
Will our airport become a spaceport?...
Will some airport nut write a book about it?

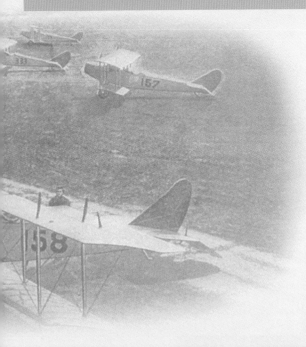

Airport of the Year
2007
Primary

Chicago Rockford International Airport
Rockford, Illinois

Presented in recognition of continued efforts in maintenance excellence and contributions to the enhancement of aviation education and community development.

 Illinois Department of Transportation
Division of Aeronautics

Susan R. Shea
Susan R. Shea, Ph.D.
Director of Aeronautics

Acknowledgments

With any book there are many people and organizations that have made it possible. Two people stand out in my mind as having led me to the point of producing this book.

Bob O'Brien: As the Executive Director of the Greater Rockford Airport he renewed my interest in aviation with his enthusiasm and outreach to the community.

Yolanda Weisensel: She and her husband, Stanley opened the Command Post restaurant in 1997. Since the restaurant building was one of the few Camp Grant buildings left, they decided to use the theme of Camp Grant... its photos and artifacts. Today their collection in the Camp Grant Museum is extensive.

Special thanks in Memory of Jon Lundin. He was the ultimate historian with a real love of Rockford and all it was and could become.

A thank you to all of the people at GRAA including Denise Delanty. She and Carol Wilcox saved me from much punctuation and spelling embarasment.

Midway Village & Museum Center for many Camp Grant photos from all eras.

Images of America Camp Grant by Gregory S. Jacobs Published by Arcadia.

Camp Grant Museum for Camp Grant photos and historical information.

Many of the photos came from the Airport archives and since the photographers are unknown we can only collectively thank them all.

Page 25 - Richard Lewis

Page 56 - Thomas Dittmar

Page 59 - Mickey Bednar (Airnikon)

Page 76 - Richard Lewis

Page 85 - Richard Lewis

Page 90 - Richard Lewis

Page 27 - Brian Thomas

Page 57 - Matt Kluck

Page 60 - Mickey Bednar (Airnikon)

Page 82 - Richard Lewis

Page 87 - Richard Lewis

Page 93 - Richard Lewis

Page 36 - Camp Grant Museum

Page 57 - Mel Lawerence

Page 61 - Bob Garrard

Page 82 - Richard Lewis

Page 88 - Richard Lewis

Page 93 - Rock Valley College

Page 43 - Brian Thomas

Page 57 - Mel Lawerence

Page 63 - Bob Garrard

Page 82 - Richard Lewis

Page 89 - Richard Lewis

Page 93 - Richard Lewis

Page 48 - Richard Lewis

Page 57 - Mel Lawerence

Page 65 - Gerald Helmer

Page 83 - Richard Lewis

Page 89 - Richard Lewis

Page 95 - Brian Thomas

Page 53 - Richard Lewis

Page 58 - Johan Ljongdahl

Page 66 - Gary Chambers

Page 83 - Richard Lewis

Page 89 - Richard Lewis

Page 96 - Brian Thomas

Page 54 - Unknown

Page 59 - Mickey Bednar (Airnikon)

Page 68 - Johan Ljungdahl

Page 83 - Richard Lewis

Page 89 - Richard Lewis

Page 97 - Brian Thomas

Page 55 - Mel Lawerence

Page 59 - Mickey Bednar (Airnikon)

Page 70 - Carlos Aleman

Page 84 - Richard Lewis

Page 90 - Richard Lewis

Page 96 - Brian Thomas

Page 99 - Gary Orlando

Page 103 - Brian Thomas

Page 108- Richard Lewis

Page 108- Richard Lewis

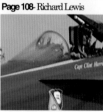

Page 108 - Richard Lewis

Page 108 - Richard Lewis

Page 109 - Richard Lewis

Page 109 - Richard Lewis

Page 109 - Richard Lewis

Page 111 - James R. Covington

Page 111- Jason Whitebird

Page 112 - Brian Thomas

Page 114 - Matt Coleman

Page 115 - Anthony Jackson

Page 116 - Richard Lewis

Many of the airline photos came from the web site:
www.airliners.net
Other web sites of interest are:
www.campgrant.org
www.midwayvillage.org
www.wingsandwheelsmuseum.org
www.emeryair.net
www.courtesyaircraft.com
www.prideaircraft.com
www.acs-rfd.com
www.airshipartistry.com
www.kaneyaerospace.com
www.avionicsplace.com
www.heritageaero.com
www.rubloffusa.com
www.morelandenterprises.com
www.airspacemag.com
www.allegiantair.com
www.flyted.com
www.flightlevel350.com
www.flytecomm.com
www.eaa.org/
www.nasm.si.edu
www.nationalmuseum.af.mil
and of course
www.flyrfd.com

CHRONOLOGY

1917: Army chooses land in New Milford Township for one of 16 training posts. The camp opened in December and cost the government $14.7 million to build.

1918: The 86th Army division with 28,000 soldiers leaves for World War I in July. In September, a Spanish influenza outbreak at Camp Grant infects 4,000 soldiers, killing 1,400 servicemen and 323 civilians.

1921: War department closes Camp Grant and puts buildings up for sale.

1924: Illinois National Guard - 33rd Division - takes over the base until 1935.

1927: Fred Machesney, a barnstorming aviator, opens Machesney Field on N. Second Street.

1940: Chicago construction company converts Camp Grant back to Army camp at a cost of $9 million.

1942: Search for new Rockford airport site. American Airlines wanted to extend service to Rockford along with Minneapolis, Dubuque and Rochester.

1943: German prisoner of war camp opens. Army closes reception center at Camp Grant.

1945: Camp Grant becomes mustering out center. Up to 25,000 per month were handled some reassigned to the pacific.

1946: President Harry Truman signs contract deeding Camp Grant to the Greater Rockford Airport Authority.

1946: First meeting of the Board of Commissioners of the Greater Rockford Airport Authority was held at the mayors office.

1947: Ground breaking for phase one of six phases.

1948: Three 4,100-foot runways constructed.

1949: Phase One completed, which included the three runways and ramp area.

1950: Federal Aviation Administration flight service station moved to Greater Rockford Airport from Machesney Airport. Charles W, Scott became first General Manager. Mid-Continent Airlines begins regular commercial service, and merged with Braniff in 1952.

1951: May 16, 1951 Ozark Airlines begins service to St. Louis.

1952: Camp Grant Officers Ballroom Building moved and remodeled into terminal.

1953: Most of the 6 phases of the initial construction completed. Charles Scott resigns. Grant Baer appointed to the job.

1954: Dedication November 1. Rockford awarded 10 daily flights by the CAB to be provided by Ozark.

1955: Grant Baer resigns. Robert Selfridge appointed. Illini Airlines begins service to Meigs Field.

1956: Construction of new maintenance hangar #2 and $160,000 control tower approved.

1957: North/South runway extend by 700 ft. VOR installed near Winnebago.

1958: June 11, 1958 Ozark boards its 100,000th passenger. Rockford Control tower becomes operational. Weather station opens on a full time basis.

1959: First EAA fly in. North Central offers twice daily service to Madison and Chicago.

1960: North/South runway extension completed.

1961: Ozark begins first Rockford service to newly opened O'Hare International Airport in Chicago. ILS goes operational in March.

1962: Peoria-Rockford bus Company begins Rockford to O'Hare Service.

1965: Runway 18-36 extended to 6,000 feet. the Northeast/southwest to 5,000 feet.

1967: New fire station, (no. 7), manned by Rockford Fire Dept, completed. Commuter Air Service begins 5 daily flights to O'Hare and Meigs in Chicago.

1971: Runway 18-36 extended to 8,200 feet.

1972: Midstates Commuter Service begins flights to Detroit. MATS, (Merchants Aviation Transport Service) offers weekday flights to Peoria and Detroit.

1974: Majority of remaining Camp Grant buildings demolished.

1977: Selfridge retires. Bill Grady is new Director. Deregulation of airlines begins. Radar installed.

1978: Tower sold to FAA. Coleman Air Transport has flights to Detroit and Minneapolis.

1980: TWA begins 727 flights to O'Hare.

1981: Confederate Air Force Show.

1982: Mississippi Valley Airlines begins flights to O'Hare, Ozark quits Rockford.

1983: Confederate Air Force Show.

1984: American Central Airlines offers three flights daily from Rockford to Detroit. Frontier Airlines begins flights to Denver.

1985: Concord arrives Oct. 1,1985.

1986: First Midwest Airfest featuring the Thunderbirds. Northwest Airlink has flights to Minneapolis/Saint Paul.

1987: Grand opening of new Terminal in September.

1988: Jim Vitale opens St. James Envoy.

1989: Emery Worldwide marks the beginning of air cargo at Rockford. Skyway Airlines offers flights to Milwaukee

1990: American Eagle flights to O'Hare begin.

1991: Annexation to the city of Rockford. .

1994: UPS opens a 500,000-square-foot sorting hub.

1996: Northwest Airlink begins flights to Detroit.

2001: Bax Global comes to airport

2002: Bob O'Brien begins as executive director.

2004: Hooters Air begins flights to Atlanta, Denver, Myrtle Beach and Las Vegas.

2005: International arrival gate facility opens. 2 new jet bridges and baggage carrousel added to terminal. Airport holds first airshow since 1991, Sunship1 offers flights to Cancun. Northwest Airlink begins service to Detroit.

2006: United Express is flying to Denver and Allegiant Air has flights to Las Vegas and Sanford, Fla. UPS is adding sorting equipment and plans to boost its seasonal employment to nearly 2,000.

Index